THE POOR GIRL'S FINANCIAL GUIDE

A Booklet of Ideas on Personal Finance

D. Kirn

Dedication

This is dedicated to my parents who have been very influential in my financial life. They have given me a solid foundation on personal finance by sharing with me financial decisions and the impact on their lives. This is also dedicated to my loving partner who has been supportive of me in the writing of this book. I am grateful for her assistance and encouragement.

A Little about Myself

I am 37 years old. Ever since I was in grade school, I've wanted to retire by the age of 40. I can tell you that this will not happen now. I've made enough mistakes along the way to severely hinder my ability to retire at 40. My goal now is to retire at 46. If I can retire at 46, I will feel successful at gaining control over my financial future. I will accomplish this by taking charge of my life and my finances using the Poor Girl method.

As I grew up, I received many lessons on money from my parents. Most of these lessons were from my father in particular. He is a big influence in my financial life. He used an approach with me that I will use with you. He told me about his good decisions and how he made them. He didn't want me to make the same mistakes he made. And I haven't, I've made completely different ones. But I've been able to apply everything he has taught me to create a solid financial foundation. In this book I will share the things that I do and why I do them.

I am not a financial advisor. I do not have a degree in accounting or finance. I am not certified in any financial services. I am not even a bookkeeper. I am an average person like you. I have a Bachelor degree in Business Management with a concentration in human resource management. I am a payroll clerk working for a payroll processing company. This does not qualify me to tell anyone how to make financial decisions.

I simply want to take you through my financial journey with the things I have learned about being proactive in the fight for financial security. I would like to teach you my philosophy and what I view as a Poor Girl way of life. I would like to share how this view of the world, through a Poor Girl's eyes, can help you to create a secure financial foundation so you can focus on building your savings and retirement investments.

I would like to show you some of the decisions I've had to make, some of the thought process I go through in making these decisions, and even what I would do if I were put into other types of situations. You will hear my opinion on money saving and making techniques. These are just my thoughts. Once you see my thoughts, you can make your own decisions. You can learn from my ideas, improve on them, and create ideas of your own. If you can do this, you will do better than me.

Choosing to Feel Poor

Ok, I would say I am not poor but I certainly feel poor. I know I am luckier than many people in this world. I have a job, which makes me luckier than millions of other individuals who are out of work. I have a place to live, with options to live elsewhere if necessary. I have a very loving and generous family, including my partner of four years. I have a vehicle to get to and from work. I have food, clothing, a computer and furniture. I have more than many people in this world have. So why do I say I feel poor?

This feeling is a choice. It feels like a lifestyle choice, a way of living life. I certainly could choose to spend every dollar that comes in and have the latest and greatest of everything. I choose not to do this. Much of this feeling is self-imposed. It is designed to help me make an opportunity to create more for my future. Making decisions as a Poor Girl has become second nature. Instead, I choose to invest in my future.

This certainly does not take away from those who are truly without and suffering in this world with little to no resources. This is a feeling created by choice, not an actual reality. The Poor Girl feeling is the way I help myself to make more by purposefully using less. It is a method I use to create long term growth and financial prosperity.

Like most of America, I don't have money for a lot of extras. I am happy to pay my bills, purchase groceries and buy some much needed clothing for work. I could have more, but I choose to give myself just enough to get by. I contribute to my 401k, give myself a budget for food and gas, and occasionally purchase stock and put money into savings for special goals. Sure, I could stop contributing to my 401k so that I could have a few hundred more each month for spending. But then what would happen to me?

I would have to work until I drop dead, or end up in the poor house on Medicaid dying alone in the worst nursing home possible in the United States. I would much rather save what I can, so that I can purchase care in a decent facility when needed. I will need money to pay someone to drive me to the store or to appointments when I am no longer a safe driver on the road. I need to make sure I can retire and that I don't run out of money when I do. I don't think I will want to go back to work at the age of 85.

Creating this Poor Girl feeling has become very motivational. I know that the more I keep my finances under control, the more I see my debts reduce and my investments grow. I see my financial security growing. I see my goal of retiring at age 46 becoming closer to reality. But I should first go step by step showing how I created this Poor Girl feeling. The Poor Girl feeling needs to be obtained by figuring out how much income I should allow myself access to. So I will call this accessible income.

My first step to cutting back on my accessible income is to figure out exactly how much money I need on a monthly basis to cover just my bills. I am not including in this gas, food, clothing, entertainment or other extras. By bills I mean mortgage payment, condo association dues, rent, water, electric, gas, telephone, car payment and insurances. These are the things that won't go away right away or some at all, although we will look at ways to cut down on their costs at a later time.

After figuring out my constant monthly expenses, I now have a figure to work from. I have a baseline to add to, subtract from, and a way to see what is extra. Now I figure out what my net pay is from my job each month. If I get paid every week, I take four pays a month. I ignore the four times a year that I get one extra check. If I get paid every two weeks, I ignore the two times a year that I get one extra check. If I get paid twice a month or monthly, I get no extra checks and have no room for error. Once I see what my net or take home pay is each month, I subtract from that the constant monthly expenses. Whatever is left is what I have to work with to squeeze out my variable expenses, extra savings and investments from.

I can also work backwards and figure out more money to defer into my 401k or other retirement plan at work. But my second step, once I figure out my net pay for each month, is to make sure that I never touch the money I need to pay my constant monthly expenses. This keeps me feeling poor and at the same time completely capable of paying my bills each month.

I know this sounds like I squeeze each month too close on paying bills. Since I put every extra dollar into investments, this is probably the impression you get. This is not the case. Early on in my career, before I started investing, I built up just enough in my checking account to have my bills paid for two months. I did this by squeezing more out of every dollar and leaving it in my checking account. Every dollar over two months of bill payments then went into extra investments and my emergency fund. Another way a Poor Girl can build this cushion is to use bonus checks or tax returns. This extra money means that I will never overdraft. I now have breathing room when I make mistakes. A Poor Girl lives poor so that she can create security for herself. She doesn't want to live paycheck to paycheck. She certainly doesn't want to live off of credit cards or pay day loans until her next pay check gets deposited.

Separating Fixed Expenses from Variable Expenses

I am a person who is capable of wasting money that comes in. So as a Poor Girl, I have to trick myself into spending less. There are many ways I do this. First, I keep multiple bank accounts open for completely separate purposes. Next, I try to make the bank account that is exclusively for paying my fixed expenses as inaccessible as possible. The other bank accounts I keep for variable expenses remain more accessible. This is how I keep control of my money as a Poor Girl. This may not work for you, but I will show you how this works for me.

I have been a member of a small bank, which currently has only five branches, since my early twenties. Since this bank is so small, I will call it Mom and Pop bank. It was close to my home at the time, but far from my place of work. This made it physically inaccessible Monday through Friday during normal business hours. The bank is open on Saturdays with limited hours. Being a lazy twenty-something, I rarely went to the bank except to make deposits of my paychecks. I also at the time, decided not to ask for a debit card. This made it inaccessible by ATM. I have online access to my account information, but my computer can't print up cash. With no debit card, I can't use it to pay for anything in person at a store.

I was later able to limit my interaction with this Mom and Pop bank even further when I took a job that offered direct deposit. So this made trips to the bank even less necessary than before. With direct deposit, there was less chance I would take a portion of my check in cash. When my new employer offered a debit card for payroll deposits, I decided to budget just enough to the debit card for food and gas, while allowing the remainder of my money to be deposited to my regular bank account. It was at this point that my bank account exclusively became an account for bill paying only.

Eventually, I decided to drop the debit card offered by my employer. I did this in favor of a great online bank. It offered a modest interest rate for a checking account with no fees. The service and options offered at this bank opened up some opportunities for creative savings. I opened a couple savings accounts with this bank. This bank also allowed me to nickname my accounts. I decided to nickname them with goals I had in mind, such as "Vacation Fund" and "Emergency Fund". The checking account I opened with the online bank provided me with a debit card to replace the one my employer offered. This account is also exclusively for gas, food and other variable expenses. I nicknamed this account "Spending Money". I connected this checking account to my bill paying account at my Mom and Pop bank. Being able to name these accounts, helps me to define exactly what each account is used for. It helps me to budget my money and take control.

The Mom and Pop bank is now exclusively getting my payroll direct deposits. I set up my online account to automatically receive deposits from my Mom and Pop bank four times a month. This is a set dollar amount I use for gas and groceries. Since I set it to automatically happen, the only thing I need to do is watch what I spend that money on to make it stretch to the next deposit. I consider this a paying "me" bill for the Mom and Pop bank.

Since I can visit my online account anytime I want, I can keep an eye on it and never run the risk of over-drafting. As circumstance would have it, I have moved farther away from my Mom and Pop bank. I refuse to change banks to make the accessibility grow. I like that it is now 18 miles away. I still do not have an ATM card to this account. I still can't go to an ATM and withdraw money or pay bank fees on this account. I have made this account very difficult to access. Plus, even 18 miles away, I have received better service from this Mom and Pop bank than I have at other big regional banks I used to bank with in the past.

In addition to my Mom and Pop bank being exclusively for bill paying, I set up most of my bills for automatic bill payment. I did not set it so the bank does the automatic payment. I set it so the businesses themselves pull the money from my bank account. I know people who think it is a good idea for the bank to make the payments. Whether real or imagined, I feel this may leave room for error and bank fees depending on your account type. If your monthly bill changes even slightly for phone use, utilities, a change in escrow for you mortgage or other change and you don't notice, then you run the risk that the bank won't pay the correct amount. Instead, the company billing you should draft the money from your bank account each month. They know how much they want from you and what day they want to receive it. You will never be charged a late fee on a bill not fully paid or paid a day late. You don't have to check your invoices to make sure you modify your payment. For me, this also means I am not personally paying a bill, accessing my account, or dipping into it for anything other than bill paying.

When bill paying becomes invisible, I am less likely to think about that account. It is out of sight and out of mind. This isn't to say that I don't know when I am erroneously billed. I still check my account to see what has come out for the month. I still know what is happening. I read my mail and know when my bills change. A Poor Girl doesn't lose control by automating. She actually gains more control over her finances.

To summarize what I've done, I need only a few sentences. I opened an account for bill paying only at a bank that would take effort to get to. I have direct deposit into this account and I do not have a debit card for this bank. I have a separate account at a separate online bank with a debit card for gas and groceries only. I keep an eye on the debit card account so that I stay within my budget for the essential bill of "me". I also automate my bill paying to think less about my accounts and reduce errors in bill payments.

If you have issues over-drafting your account or just plain spending too much, consider trying my tick with inaccessibility. It's possible this method or some variation will work for you. Certainly, it can help a Poor Girl gain more control over her finances.

How the Poor Girl Pays for College

We all know college is expensive. There are many ways to pay for college. I know that the way I paid for college is not necessarily the way everyone else should. Even so, I am going to show you the way I financed my college education. I'll even tell you other options I explored. None of which involved risking my parent's financial health. This is the Poor Girl's way to pay for college when she has no choice but to pay for it herself.

Scholarships are the first option to explore. I am not the smartest person in the world. I don't have any athletic ability. I have not participated in any special activity that would qualify for a scholarship. Even so, I still looked for scholarships as a senior in high school. Now I hear it might even be smart to start looking as soon as junior year. My school had postings for various scholarships; I qualified for none of them. I went to the library, back when people actually read paper books. I looked to see if there was some obscure scholarship for five foot tall girls with freckles who are polish, but found none. I did, however, take the ACT test. Lucky for me, I got a score that was just barely high enough to qualify for a $1K scholarship for my first year of college education. Unfortunately, I did poorly enough my first year of college that it didn't extend into my second year.

The point here is you may think you don't qualify for one, but you should look anyway. Even a small scholarship that saves you some money will help you on the road to financial security. Why pass up a chance to reduce your costs?

Federal student guaranteed loans are another option to explore. My second year of post high school education, I left college in favor of a trade school. It was one year of intensive training. How did I pay for this? I mostly paid with a guaranteed loan. There are those that look at student loans as a thing of evil. Something to rack up debt before you even have a real career. I don't look at it this way. As long as you are smart, try to keep them to a minimum, and have a plan to pay the loans off. They are a means to an end. It also saves your parents from losing the shirts off their backs while trying to pay for your education. Many people may not have parents willing or even able to kick in for their education, and they shouldn't have to. Either way, it helps you to get what you need to become the person you want to be with the career of your choosing.

Try working a full or part time job while in school. I worked both full and part time jobs to help pay for my tuition through my post high school education. This money went to my books, gas, food and tuition. Working helped me pay off my student loans, reduce the amount of loans I needed, and helped me to pay for my trade school diploma, Associates degree and Bachelor's degree. I feel no shame for having paid for much of my education.

Look for an employer with tuition reimbursement. Most small businesses aren't going to offer this to you. If you are looking for a job, look to the bigger corporations for tuition reimbursement. As a young person looking for experience, working in the mailroom or the reception desk for tuition reimbursement is not such a bad idea. Some companies require you to remain in their employ for a number of years after your last tuition reimbursement. If you don't, you may have to repay the money. If you are ok with this and can stick it out with your employer, it's a great way to pay for your college. This helped me to pay for exactly half my tuition when I went back to school to finish my bachelor's degree. The other half I paid with my salary from working for them.

Other options are also on the table. If I wasn't making enough money and didn't want to rack up student loans, I would have cut my college education down to part time and worked on finishing my education slowly. I would have also completed more of the basics at a community college, which is cheaper per credit hour. Sometimes you can cut expenses on books by buying used. As a Poor Girl in college, I lived at home with my parents for many years instead of on campus. There are many ways to cut expenses and pay for college. You just have to find the right mix for you. There is a way that everyone can afford a college education. You just have to find your way.

Getting Your Retirement Plans in Place

Once you get your expenses, education, and bill paying under control, retirement becomes the next concern. You've taken care of your immediate concerns. Now you need to think about your future. A Poor Girl doesn't want to work forever, unless it's by choice. She does everything in her power to give herself every chance to retire. She doesn't depend on social security, money that may or may not be there when she reaches retirement age. A Poor girl wants to take her retirement into her own hands and doesn't leave it to chance.

The first thing a Poor Girl does is explore retirement investment vehicles. The best place to start is with your employer. Find out if your employer offers a 401K, 403 (b), Simple IRA or other plans that you are eligible to participate in. You may find that if you are new to this employer, you may not be eligible to participate unless you have been there for a certain length of time, are full time, or some other requirement your company has. The important thing is to find out what they offer, if you are eligible, and how fast you can begin contributing.

You also need to know if your employer will match any or all of your contributions. Make sure you contribute at least the minimum you need to in order to get the entire matching contribution. A Poor Girl doesn't pass up free money. That's just silly! Passing up the match is like telling your employer you don't want a raise. Why would you do that? You work hard. You should let your employer pay you for it…even if you don't get to use the money until you retire.

If there is no match, consider contributing to the plan anyway. If you can't seem to save for yourself, let them take the money and invest it for you before you even see it. There is less chance you won't be prepared for your retirement. If you have to wait a year before you are eligible to participate in your employer's plan, you may want to set aside the money you were planning on contributing into an emergency fund, paying off debt faster, or investing in your own IRA. It is up to you what you do with it. A Poor Girl, in this position, will just try to make a decision she thinks will get her closer to her goals.

If you have an employer that doesn't offer a retirement plan, this is no excuse to ignore your retirement. A Poor Girl takes charge of her situation and her future. She opens an IRA at a discount brokerage or bank. She doesn't even need to walk into a bank. She can open one online with a reputable established company. She does her research when choosing an institution for her retirement investments. She researches fees, minimum starting investments and investment choices within an IRA.

Once a Poor Girl decides to open an IRA she needs to decide what kind, a Traditional IRA or a Roth IRA. I won't go into too much detail here because I am not an expert by any means on what is the best. I will say I like the Roth IRA very much because the money a Poor Girl invests is after-tax dollars, out of her own pocket. The money earned in a Roth IRA is tax free when deducted at retirement. So it is tax free retirement income. Sweet, isn't it?

This Poor Girl knows a lot of people who tell her they can't afford to invest or save because their expenses are too high. These people can't seem to put an extra $100 into a Roth IRA. They also have no motivation to find out how to set up an account or learn about stocks. If you are one of these people, then let your employer do it for you. Don't give up your retirement because you don't want to open a Roth IRA. The point here is you need to decide what you are capable of doing. Whatever that is, you need to work around that to manipulate your money behaviors to ensure you invest enough of your income to retire. You do have the money to save. Just be willing to find ways to cut expenses to do it.

Sometimes we need to get creative to fund our retirement investments. Sometimes we need to simplify. Here are some creative and not-so-creative ways to help fund your retirement and to make it grow faster.

• A young Poor Girl starts her retirement as soon as she is hired by her employer, so she never misses money she never had in her pocket.

• Fund your retirement at least enough to get the full matching contribution. Don't pass up free money.

• When you get raises, increase your contribution to your retirement plan. This is an easy way to increase contributions without feeling a pinch.

• Scale back vacations and other big purchases. Look for deals. Use the money to fund your Roth IRA or other retirement account.

• If you rent, can you find a comparable apartment or house for less rent money? How about getting a roommate to share the rent with? Use that monthly savings to fund your retirement.

• Find other daily expenses to cut back on. As a Poor Girl, I found there are many places to cut corners. Find stuff you can do without, or with less of. A Poor Girl takes that savings and put it into her retirement fund.

• Lastly, a Poor Girl never dips into her 401k by taking a 401K loan. This is the quickest way to potentially lose out on growth opportunities for her 401K investment money. If she needs a down payment for a house, she saves for it another way. Even if it means she has to wait.

Nothing bothers this Poor Girl more than people who say they can't afford to save for retirement. People can't afford to ignore their retirement. Everyone can find a way to squeeze a few dollars out of their current expenses to save for retirement. If that means making your own coffee or drinking office coffee instead of going to the local coffee joint, then do it. Instead of going out for dinner at an Italian restaurant for $30, make pasta at home for $5. That extra $25 can add up fast. I bet you will have left overs the next day, saving you even more. Take a lunch from home to work every day. That's another $5 each day you save for a total of $25 a week. That's $1300 a year. And don't get me started on the people that have to take a $4k vacation every year. What in the world are they thinking choosing a vacation over retirement? Apparently, they want to work forever. Why not plan wisely and cut the vacation expense in half? Put $2K in your Roth and use the other $2K for a decent vacation. And even better, take a vacation every 3 years and do staycations the other two years.

I think once a person sees just how large retirement savings can get from some simple lifestyle changes, it will encourage them to make additional changes to save more. Believe me they can grow fast. Why cheat your future just to have instant gratification? Cut back on the things you want now, to have the things you need later. This is the Poor Girl way of life.

Ok, so now I have told you my opinion, but have I put it to work in my own life? I have a 401K through my employer. When I began working there, I started contributing right away. My employer's plan allowed this at the time. I contributed enough to receive the full match offered by my employer. Over the years I have increased my contributions. Sometimes, not always, I put my raises into my 401K. Sometimes I increased my contributions by cutting back on my expenses. I do cheaper vacations and have skipped vacations some years. And yes, I also have a Roth IRA as a supplement to my retirement plan.

The Poor Girl's Emergency Fund

Everyone needs an emergency fund. There are many situations we get into where an emergency fund is necessary. You never know when your car will break down, the roof needs to be replaced, or you lose your job. I've used my emergency fund to cover car repairs more than a couple times. Nothing is worse than using a credit card and never paying it off. Emergency debt does not feel good. And it doesn't easily go away.

Unfortunately, many of us don't have enough of an emergency fund built up, myself included. Many people say we need to have anywhere from 6 months to a year's worth of wages in an emergency fund. The idea behind this is that if you lose your job, you have time to find a job before you become homeless or have your car repo'd. Unemployment benefits are only a portion of our earned wages, so it helps us pay our monthly bills. It can give a person some breathing room, so they can focus on finding their next job.

Admittedly, this is my weakness as a Poor Girl. I struggle to save because I find it too tempting to put every extra dollar into investments. Slowly but surely, I have managed to create a modest emergency fund.

Before you decide how to fund your emergency fund, you need to decide what bank you will use. You need to decide if it will it be a savings account or money market account. Do you want to write checks out of the account? That would be a money market account. Personally, I want my savings to be inaccessible. Having a money market would make it easier for me to dip into my emergency fund, making it harder to save and keep money in it. This is not the account for me. See what kind of rates you can get with a savings account versus a money market. I am not an expert on these two types of accounts.

Regarding banks, my recommendation is to shop around. The one thing I do see through my own research is that the online banks typically appear to have better interest rates on savings accounts than local bank branches. My savings account is through an online bank. I really like the online bank I use. I personally feel the rate I am getting is good for this type of account. I also feel the service I get from the online bank is excellent. While a Poor Girl is concerned with interest rates, sometimes considering the level of service and other benefits of a bank can overrule the importance of an interest rate. It is something a Poor Girl needs to decide for herself.

There are many ways to set up an emergency fund. The first way is a set it and forget it method. After you figure out your expenses and what you need to live, figure out how much you can spare to save. Set up automatic deposits to a savings or money market account. Some banks allow you to have the money transferred automatically from your checking account into your savings account on a specific date each month. In this way, it can become similar to bill paying. You know it will happen like paying a bill each month. The amount remains the same, unless you change it. Since you set it up automatically, the bank takes care of the rest. You don't have to do a thing after that unless you want to change the deposit amounts or deposit frequency.

A second option for an automatic deposit is through your employer. Most medium size and large size businesses offer direct deposit. Even some smaller employers offer it as a benefit too. If your employer offers direct deposit, you can set up an automatic deposit with each paycheck to be deposited into your emergency fund. This makes it an easy way to save without much effort.

The third way to set up an emergency fund is a self-directed method. What this means is that a Poor Girl develops the self-discipline to direct any extra funds she has into an emergency fund. So she makes the deposits herself. She may direct bonus checks into an emergency fund. If she is paid weekly, four times a year she may direct the fifth paycheck in a month to her emergency fund. If she is paid bi-weekly, she may direct an additional pay two times a year into her emergency fund. She might deposit her income tax refund towards emergencies. She might even keep a change jar and deposit the change that builds up into the bank once a year. It could be anything. A Poor Girl looks for any clever or ordinary way to save. The main thing is a Poor Girl finds the extra money and puts it away for a rainy day. She finds more pleasure in saving than in spending.

As a Poor Girl myself, I get excited about finding extra money to either save or invest. It makes me feel better to see the results from saving and investing, than in spending. I believe that any shopaholic can be reformed if they save for a significant period of time and see the tangible benefits. A person can learn to love saving as much as shopping. We just need to start doing it. Over time saving money can become second nature. But we need a place start. Find a bank with a decent interest rate and then look for ways to fund it. It is important that a Poor Girl decide what methods she will use. A Poor Girl must continue to find new ways to save money if she ever hopes to have an adequate emergency fund. A Poor Girl doesn't depend on credit cards to get her through an emergency.

Extra Ideas for a Poor Girl to Save Money

As a Poor Girl I've found various ways to save through trial and error. I'm sure you will find your own ways to save too. Maybe you can find some useful tips here to help you save money and turbo charge your retirement plans. You might even be able to improve on the ideas included here with your own.

• Don't smoke. That is the biggest waste of money ever. First of all, there is no nutritional value. It sucks up a ton of your money both for the cigarette pack and the taxes on it. Second, it could cost you tons in co-pays and hospital stays when you get a myriad of cigarette related illnesses and diseases. This is something that will prevent anyone from getting ahead in life. Show me a smoker and I will show you someone who won't retire early.

• Don't go overboard on air conditioning. Wherever possible, just open the windows and use the fans. Go visit family or friends who would love to see you and don't mind you breathing in their cool air conditioning. When it's a really hot day, close doors and vents to rooms that you don't use often. This will help conserve energy so you are only keeping a few rooms cool instead of the whole house. Use thick curtains on windows that get a lot of heat and sunlight to block out some of the heat. Plant a tree near next to your house for additional shade.

• In the cold winter months, the same concept used for air conditioning can be applied to heating your house. Close off rooms you don't use often by closing doors and vents. Turn the dial down two degrees and wear a sweater. Spend a little money to replace drafty windows and get the energy credit on your tax returns. In the long run, your wallet will thank you for it.

• Replace old light bulbs with energy efficient light bulbs. This can really reduce your electric bill. Over time, the savings will add up.

• Do you need premium channels? Can you cut your bill by getting rid of them? What stations do you watch the most? Can you just get a converter box and get rid of the cable all together? Many of our favorite shows can be watched on the internet for free. Before I moved in with my partner, I got rid of my cable and used a converter box. I even watched special programs I missed with my parents when I visited them. I saved a lot of money!

• Can you modify your phone plan? Do you use all your minutes? See if you can cut this down. Does your employer have a discount program with a phone company? By the way, I have a flip phone. Don't laugh; I use a computer for my internet. I use a cell phone to talk and text only. Last time I modified my cell phone plan I saved approximately $30 a month. What about a prepaid plan? I have a friend who pays approximately $100 per year for just enough minutes to last the year. If she ends up needing more, she can buy more. It is much cheaper for her than a phone plan.

• Keep your tires properly inflated, it will help your mileage. Read your owner's manual or talk to your mechanic about this. I can tell it makes a big difference in miles per gallon every time a big adjustment is made on my tires.

• I only get my oil changed every 4000 to 5000 miles. I am not a mechanic, but my grandfather was one. He told me to wait because the oil is still good at 3000 on my vehicle. So before you make a decision on this, talk to a mechanic you trust to see what they say and follow their advice. Following my grandfather's advice has saved me a ton of money over the years in service fees.

•   Do you need a land line? If you don't need one to have internet access and you primarily use your cell phone for communication, consider getting rid of it. It is just a big waste of money, if you make most or all of your phone calls on your cell phone.

•   Why stop in the morning at a coffee shop for coffee or tea on your way to work? Drink office coffee or make it at home before you leave for the day. If you like tea, go buy a box of your favorite flavor and make it yourself. That's what I do and I love my tea.

•   Why not make your lunch for work instead of eating out? You can save a ton of money this way. It might also be a way to lose weight by eating healthier and staying away from fast food.

•   Don't waste your left-overs; eat them for dinner the next day. It stretches your money even farther. I love my left-overs, because then I don't have to cook.

•   If you have the talent, and I don't, try making some of your holiday gifts. Some homemade gifts I have received in the past include blankets, mixed CDs, and as a child a hand sewn doll. Gifts I managed to make include a scrap book for my partner, a picture inserted into a frame I decorated, T-shirts decorated by me, and poetry.

•   Sometimes I get compliments on my shoes, which I find funny. I won't say where I shop because I am not advertising for anyone, but I never pay more than $15 for a pair of shoes. In fact, I usually pay less than $12. There are very few places that carry my size and fortunately for me those stores are not called Pay More or Not-O-K mart. I look for deals, sometimes buy one get one half off, clearance, and sometimes they are just low-price less than $12 not-on-sale shoes.

• When purchasing clothes online, I try to get free shipping with a discount code. You can use a search engine online to look for discount codes. If there isn't a discount shipping code, there may be a discount code on the merchandise itself.

• When purchasing clothes in the store, I try to stick to the clearance section. I like end of season sales with huge clearance sections. These are fun. I don't walk out with a lot, but occasionally I do find a diamond in the rough. I love it when I find shirts for work that are less than $5. But trust me, as a Poor Girl I stay out of the stores as often as possible. So when I do go I get a double thrill, a shopping trip where I challenge myself to spend as little as possible on some nice merchandise.

• Consider generics. Try them once. If you can't get used to it, then buy the name brand. I bet through trial and error you will find some products you can substitute with generics. It can end up saving you tons of money. I have severe allergies and use allergy medicines every day. I only use generics for this because the key ingredients are the same and they do the same thing.

• Buy products you use a lot in bulk. Again, I go back to my allergy medicine. The over-the-counter medicine I use the most I buy a year supply of. When buying this way, the price per tablet goes down dramatically, saving a ton of money in the long run. Pick the products you use the most and find a way to buy them in bulk. Just be careful to watch expiration dates. There is no point buying the product if you can't use it all before the expiration date.

• Learn to give yourself a manicure and pedicure. Do you really need to pay a professional for that? You might not do as good a job, but practice makes perfect.

• Pay down your debt as fast as you can. Credit cards and student loans cost you money. For every dollar you pay off faster, you save a lot of interest. Many credit cards carry a high interest rate, far higher than the interest rate on a home loan. Student loans are not dischargeable in bankruptcy. Credit cards and student loans should be the first thing you pay off to save money.

• Buying a car? Consider buying a used car. Maybe purchase a car that was a lease and only two or three years old. Check around for the best rate on a car loan if you can't pay cash. Don't just have the dealer help you apply for a loan. Do it yourself to see what is out there. Credit unions have great rates. My Mom and Pop bank gave me a great rate on a car loan when I allowed them to automatically deduct the loan payment from my checking account each month. The dealer was impressed when I told them the rate I was getting. They couldn't have gotten that for me.

• Don't be loyal to an insurance company. Get quotes at least every two or three years from at least two companies. If you don't, you will most likely see your insurance rates continue to climb. I find that when I do this, I save on my car insurance anywhere from $25 - $100 when switching. Same thing goes for home owners' insurance, check around. Deals won't appear out of thin air. Sometimes a couple hours of work are worth the savings.

• Talk with your family and friends to see if you can borrow books and DVDs from them. Then you aren't buying books on your own or upgrading to the premium channels on T.V.

• Find people at work that live close to you. See if you can car pool with them a few times a week. It saves on gas money.

- Find a generic dog biscuit your dogs like just as much and the name brand. Then see if you can get this kind at a discount store.

- Unplug your toaster and other non-essential appliances when not in use.

- Teach yourself new skills that can save you money. The biggest thing I did for myself was to learn how to sew. I watched an online video about how to hem pants. I am very short and nearly everything I buy has to be hemmed. I used to pay someone $10 - $12 to hem a pair of pants or jeans. Now I can do it myself. By extension, I have also learned to sew holes closed in older clothing so I can make them last longer. I hate throwing away a sweater that has an easy to repair hole. I no longer bother my mother to sew on buttons for me. I also sew on the patches on my partner's uniform, so she doesn't have to pay a seamstress to do it. Other ideas for you: If you get your eye brows waxed professionally, learn to pluck your own. Learn to dye or highlight your own hair. Learn to bake your own cake instead of buying one. Just teach yourself new skills so you don't have to pay someone else to do it.

- Certain fruits are cheap like bananas and apples. Consider adding more of these to your diet. It fills you up, is nutritious and cheap too.

- Looking for a fun hobby, grow your own tomatoes and strawberries. Why buy these in a store when you can be cheap and grow them yourself? These are even plants you can grow on your terrace if you are in an apartment.

- Before you buy anything you need, check with family and friends to see if they have it and don't need it. You might find them handing it over to you for cheap or for nothing at all.

• Looking for something fun to do? Many activities don't cost a dime. Take a walk, go to a park, play catch with your kids/nieces/nephews, do some gardening, go window shopping, tan in your back yard the natural way, go bike riding, bird watching, people watching. Replace an activity you pay for with something that is free to do. Make it a weekly/daily thing for you. This is a great way to curb spending.

• A Poor Girl doesn't make impulse purchases. She waits a few days to make sure she still really wants it. Try this technique. If you've forgotten about it, it wasn't important enough to waste your money on. You are better off saving it instead.

Do you really need the latest and greatest of everything? I don't. I don't want to leave myself with no sense of security and no possible path to retirement. I don't want to work forever. If you feel this way too, then don't cut yourself short later on to have "it" now. "It" won't last as long as you do, I promise. Then later on, you will be wondering why you have nothing. It is because you used it up years ago to buy something you don't have anymore. Don't create a bad situation for yourself. Fight the urge to splurge. Only purchase necessities as you need them. Treat yourself, you deserve it. But if you do, look for deals and ways to do everything cheaper.

Use your head, get creative and think about all purchases for a week before you make them. You might talk yourself out of spending a few dollars. Talk with your friends and family. Maybe they know a way you can get what you are looking for at a discount rate. Maybe they will have one they don't use and can give to you. Sometimes other people know things you don't know. I've found I missed out on saving money by not asking around first. A Poor Girl takes charge of her finances and searches for ways to save money.

Poor Girls Find Ways to Make Money

Poor Girls look for more ways to make money. Some ways are conventional and some not so conventional. I'm not just talking about working a full time job. I'm talking about making your full time job pay you more, making money outside of work, generating money on things you have and coming up with ways to create a continuous income.

Living like a Poor Girl does not mean a Poor Girl doesn't live like a worker bee. She does everything she can to make more money, not just make her money stretch. As she makes more money, she also makes her money work for her and her future.

Ok, so say you are one of the lucky ones with a full time job. Does your employer offer you opportunity to earn incentives for performance? Many medium and larger size employers offer the opportunity to earn bonus pay based on performance. Say you sell more than your quota you get a bonus…well then, work extra or develop new leads to sell more. What about keeping costs down, cutting company losses, exceeding your employer tracked statistical expectations? Whatever incentives your company offers, exceed them to earn more.

Are you hourly, salary or commission? Can you ask your employer to let you work overtime? If commission, can you increase your sales by using new techniques? Get with higher-performing employees and ask them how they sell more. Ask them to tell you what they think are good techniques in customer service and sales. Don't think that people are unwilling or unable to help you. You never know until you try asking. I've found my coworkers to be very informative when asked for help. People want you to succeed. When you succeed, the entire company succeeds. This means more job stability for all. Look to your more efficient coworkers to learn to work smarter. Don't be ashamed to ask for help. It shows ambition to do better.

What about negotiating with your employer to earn higher commissions on your larger sales? It doesn't hurt to ask. The worst they can say to you is no. Just don't walk in there without a reason. Tell them how you can earn more money for the company by working overtime hours. Let them know how you will increase company earnings by increasing your productivity, if they will allow you to earn a higher rate of commission. Have your logical reasons listed, come prepared, and you will either be given what you ask for or some other benefit you weren't expecting. You won't know until you ask.

Do you get annual reviews and a chance to earn a raise? Talk with your boss before your review. Ask him/her what you can do to make yourself more valuable to the company and to prove your worth. This is a direct approach that they will respect. It is an approach I have used, and it did get me more money. My employer told me exactly what I could do to make myself more valuable to the company. I followed my boss's advice and became more respected by upper management. My supervisor's manager made sure I got a bigger raise on more than one occasion, as did my supervisor fight to get me more money. This continues to happen, five years after I first took her advice.

Make money outside of work. What are your talents? Can you use them to make a few bucks here or there? If I can become even better at hemming and mending, maybe I can charge a few dollars to do that for other people. I've heard of people who shovel their neighbor's driveways and sidewalks in the winter for extra money. What about cleaning houses on the weekend? There are online services where people can connect with others for child care. What about using an online service to find work as a babysitter? Only you know yourself best. What could you do to earn a few extra dollars that you wouldn't mind doing? I'm great at writing letters and pinching pennies. I've decided to try writing a book to see what that gets me.

Generate money on the things you already have. What do you have, that you don't use, that someone else may want to buy or rent? I have a few ideas on the matter. Some of them I've done, some I will do in the future, and some I've seen others do.

• Selling your house? Ask your agent if they will drop their commission by 1%. This will help you keep more of what you sell your house for. If your agent won't do it, find another. Don't sign on with an agent until you negotiate this point. It isn't fair to you or the agent to start working together when you don't tell them what you are looking for right from the beginning.

• Selling your car? Sell it yourself. Don't trade it in unless it is a real junker. You will get more money if you sell it yourself. There are online resources you can reference to see what you get if you trade it in versus selling it yourself. Just plug in the information about your car and it will do the rest of the work. It provides the information to help you decide on a selling price.

• Donate the things you don't sell in your garage sale to charity. It won't be money in your pocket right away, but it can help with your tax return when you write off the donation amount. Plus, you have the pleasure of helping someone in need.

• Have a vacation home? What about renting it out when it is not in use? Other people might like to vacation there as well. Better yet, sell the vacation home and get a hotel like everyone else. It is cheaper than a second mortgage, property tax and all the upkeep that goes into a property you only use a few weeks a year. A Poor Girl wouldn't really consider owning a vacation home if she truly wants to put all her energy into securing her future.

• Underwater on your home? Unable to sell? What about renting it out so someone else pays your mortgage? You can hire a property management company to take care of it, collect the rent, and go to court for you if there are any renter problems. Just make sure you have a place to live. If you don't, do you have a room you aren't using? Maybe you can just rent out that one room to someone you trust.

• Some people hold annual garage sales. It can bring in a few dollars and help you get your spring cleaning done. Get with others you know to hold the sale together. Make it a bigger event and then advertise with signs and even place an ad. If people know you are having a two or three family garage sale, they are more likely to come knowing there is more to browse.

This brings me to my last thoughts about generating money. Investing in stocks that pay dividends can be a way you generate money without having to work for it. When I purchase stocks and receive dividends, I feel like I'm making my money work for me. Of course, you would have to buy enough to generate a decent size income. So a Poor Girl squeezes as much of her unused income into buying stocks as possible. I won't advise you on which stocks are great picks or how to decide which stocks to buy. I am not qualified for that.

As I stated earlier, I am not a financial advisor or stock broker. You will either have to educate yourself or find a professional to educate you on purchasing stocks. It is important you know about the companies you are buying into. What I will tell you is that I put as much of my money into dividend paying stocks as possible and I hold on to them. I also let the dividends automatically reinvest into purchasing more stock that generates more dividends. I hope that by doing so, I will eventually earn enough money in dividends each year that I can retire in my mid-40s. How successful I am remains to be seen. As a Poor Girl, I will keep trying.

The Poor Girl Doesn't Sabotage Herself

It has been this Poor Girl's experience that people tend to try to fix other people's problems. For some, it is loaning money to friends. For others, it's bailing out their adult children. For other people, it is bending over backwards to support an unmarried partner who made poor decisions. To one degree or another, we have all been asked to help someone. A Poor Girl is careful who she helps. She doesn't just help anyone. She thinks about the person's circumstances, how they are related to her, and if she feels they are trying to take advantage of her.

A Poor Girl doesn't sabotage herself by bailing out an irresponsible person, they won't ever learn. Human nature is repetition. It can take a lot for someone to learn from their mistakes. A Poor Girl doesn't want to be placed in the same situation over and over. A Poor Girl gives the tools to show someone how to bail themselves out, if they will listen. If she does loan money out, she does it knowing she will probably never see the money again. If she gets it back, then it is a pleasant surprise. She also makes it known, that it is the only time they will receive financial help. If they come back asking for help later on, she makes an excuse and says no. A Poor Girl does everything she can to offer help that won't place a strain on her finances.

When loaning out money, a Poor Girl doesn't give out more than she can spare. She does not dip into her retirement accounts. She doesn't take out 401K loans. She knows this will reduce her earning power down the road. Even if that money is replaced, it already limits the growth she would have received on the investment. A Poor Girl does not dip into her emergency money for someone else's emergency. She knows that she needs to protect herself in the event of a job loss or other emergency. She doesn't want to place herself in a situation where she has to beg someone else for a loan because she gave all her money away.

A Poor Girl doesn't carry a credit card balance. If she does, then she works hard to pay that balance down. Most people at one point or another have turned to credit cards for unexpected expenses. Most of us have even used credit for non-essential purchases. Gaining control over credit card debt should be a Poor Girl's priority. The goal is to learn to use cash or debit for food, clothing, gas, and other expenses.

Why would anyone want to pay interest, years down the road on a meal at a restaurant eaten a year ago? Or maybe you want to pay interest on gas that your car used up 30,000 miles ago? How about paying for a vacation 10 years later? Doesn't seem right, does it? A Poor girl pays her credit balances down as fast as she can to end the vicious cycle of credit card debt.

There are other little ways that we all sabotage ourselves. All the little things add up. The best thing I've done as a Poor Girl is to take my time making decisions. I've tried to curb impulse purchases. I plan meals ahead and make lists to limit buying unnecessary extras. As a Poor Girl, I stay out of high-end stores. I look for deals at the big box stores. I've driven the same car for over 8 years. A Poor Girl plans and stretches every dollar she spends. She doesn't give it away and have nothing to show for it.

The Poor Girl Looks to the Future

As a Poor Girl, I always look to the future. As the future changes so do I. A Poor Girl always looks for new ways to save money, invest more, and change her plans to enable her to have a successful retirement. The worst thing a Poor Girl can do is ignore changes the economy and other environmental factors have on retirement planning. This would place a Poor Girl at a severe disadvantage. The Poor Girl keeps the behaviors that work for her, discards those that don't, and adopts new ones.

The Poor Girl looks forward to a secure retirement and does everything she can to make it happen. She doesn't let someone else's irresponsibility keep her from reaching her goals. Creating security both now and in the future is her mission. Good luck to you and to all the Poor Girls in your life and never give up.